T0162656

FOOD *for* THOUGHT

Why We Serve

Prince Tippy

Order this book online at www.trafford.com
or email orders@trafford.com

Most Trafford titles are also available at major online book retailers.

blogger/creative writer/inventor-- writers blog list: digitaldoodlesandmind-farts.blogspot.
com, chassisdetailing.blogspot.com, evelynsmeals.blogspot.com, evelynsquickmeals.
blogspot.com, theladiesarmory.blogspot.com, dude1323.blogspot.com--

Print information available on the last page.

ISBN: 978-1-4669-6691-8 (sc)
ISBN: 978-1-4669-6692-5 (hc)
ISBN: 978-1-4669-6693-2 (e)

Library of Congress Control Number: 2012921114

Trafford rev. 08/13/2018

www.trafford.com

North America & international
toll-free: 1 888 232 4444 (USA & Canada)
phone: 250 383 6864 ✦ fax: 812 355 4082

CONTENTS

Military

Faith

Martial arts

Romance

The ladies armory logo

WEDNESDAY, MAY 23, 2012

--birthday wishes (gift still pending)--

i had meant to post this a few weeks ago,
found time today--

i would like to wish "Njang28612" a happy 22nd birthday,
and many, many, more to come . . .
may the future hold great times, and good memories,
for you, and those you love--

--best wishes, prince tippy--

THURSDAY, JULY 14, 2011

--audio--

i was just think'in, if i had a
wish granted for my blog, it would
be to have robert duvall (rd) narrate,
so it might be easy for the blind
to enjoy--

so far, no followers, no money . . .
anyway, he would do the piece justice i
think . . . i might like morgan freeman(mf)
to narrate a few as well, or perhaps
jean reno(reno)--

will that happen, probably not,
but when you play ball, and you're at bat,
    --"swing for the fences"--

(i labeled the posts (mf) for morgan freeman,
(rd) for robert duvall, and (reno) for jean reno,
in case they decide to narrate for the blind
on this blog)--

    --prince tippy--

(rd)

Monday, July 11, 2011

--*good writing*--

good writing, it isn't so much
the writer, as it's the circumstances--

the cartoon coyote who's always chasing
that silly bird had a novel in him for sure . . .
so many boulders, and long falls, a "tear-jerker"
in the making(hemingway with fur i imagine)--
anyway . . . listen, observe, both yourself,
and others--
"the pen, is mightier than the sword",
only when wielded by a sharp mind, and
a good listener--

--prince tippy--

(rd)

OUR NATION

Monday, September 20, 2010

--the birth of our nation--

i wrote this on the fourth of july, 2010

--the birth of our nation--

from fertile lands,
with *endless* possibilities, and an idea,
forged from strife, and hardship,
they were joined, and a miracle happened . . .
            --freedom--

            --god bless america--

(mf)

TUESDAY, JULY 5, 2011

--the shot heard around the world--

something i wrote yesterday--

another fourth of july . . .
family, fun, freedom, the american
way--
we do it different, our *own* style of
living, a culture that welcomes new
things, and *defends* the freedom
to try them--
a special place, with creative people,
where *real* change can happen--

--prince tippy--

(mf)

TUESDAY, SEPTEMBER 11, 2012

--a day to remember (sept 11)--

i noticed the date today, and had these thoughts, with some feelings--

sept-11 . . .

a day of great loss, when hard feelings, and ill-intentions met an engineering marvel, filled with our best and brightest . . . no good point was made, instead a ball was started rolling, that has yet to find level . . . heavy loss, created unyielding intent, that terror shall not rule the land . . .

--prince tippy--

(mf)

FRIDAY, JULY 1, 2011

--it's good to be king--

all dialed in, here's what's up--

coming of age, a man sailing heavy
waters . . . be it a raft, or a yacht, matters
not--
a master of his own destiny(and a few
others), carefully chosen . . . fully trusted--
--ship, captain, crew--
(over the ocean, or to the bottom)

--ooh-rah--

(mf)

TUESDAY, JULY 5, 2011

--mutiny--

i wrote this the other day while
enjoying some coffee, at one of
my favorite spots--

trouble . . . not only brewing, but
boiling over--
the silver lining while putting
down such rebellion, is the hands-on
experience of sending a few
problems off the plank--
"swab the deck, or feed the sharks",
is often life's reality . . . but what is life,
without some adversity--
--the plank stays, the mutineers go,
the *older* the ship, the smoother the plank--
(the captain may be important, but our nations
values are at the helm, our beliefs set the course . . .
the plank has *no* love for anyone, sailing the
ship, or swabbing the deck)--

--(a happy independence day to all)--

--ooh rah--

(mf)

THURSDAY, JULY 14, 2011

--the clapper--

wrote this yesterday, still relevant
today(reader dependent) . . . :o)

a funny phrase, and two claps, is
all it takes to dominate the living room
from the couch--
the master of all things, for less than
a king's ransom, so *easy* a child could,
and routinely does, do it--
if only other of life's challenges might
be overcome so easily . . . sadly, no, turning
off the lights, and becoming "CEO", have
vastly different skill levels needed to achieve
the desired results--
--what comes easily, often goes quickly--

--prince tippy--

(mf)

WEDNESDAY, FEBRUARY 9, 2011

--the world as we know it--

i pieced this together today(over
coffee), from two letters i wrote many
years ago to my pastor . . . probably
unsent--

your values, what are they?, where
did they come from?, some learned, some
due to experience, hardships, happy times,
or faith--
experience(life's hard lessons), they
seem to *really* shape us . . . *all* too often, it's
what, or *whom*, we *think* has harmed us,
or our loved ones, and *how*, that brings
us to where we are today--
the hardships . . . needn't happen to our
neighbors, unless we let them--
my grandparents would say, "we are
as safe as the tragedies we let fall on
our neighbors", or, "turning a blind eye
to everything, means no-one will see what
happens to you some day", they were
part of the "greatest generation", a group
filled to the brim, with wisdom of *all* kinds--
so, when to act on an injustice, and
what to do about it, is often in the hands of
the heart, or the heavens . . .

yes, there is a fine line between being a
hero, and a jerk--
   sometimes, no right answer is possible,
but something must be done--
   life isn't lived as *fully* from the sidelines, these
days when there's trouble, people come running(mostly
to watch, take pictures, or gather artifacts to sell on ebay),
but *not* to get involved--
   today, most people say "i'm glad it's not me",
when they see something bad happen . . . seems to
be the *unofficial* mantra of the last few generations . . .
not cool--
   it's *great* to make a buck, but i prefer it be in an
honourable way--
   capitalism, and morality, are not one road, but
two, and it's at these crossroads, where they meet,
that we are at our best . . .
   freedom, without *morality*, is a type of *hell* to
be avoided--
   make a difference, follow your heart, be yourself . . .
go in a *good* way(change the world)--

               --best wishes to all--

(rd)

MONDAY, MARCH 7, 2011

--a nod to the north woods--

i noticed a canadian flag
today while I was walking,
i paused to reflect on our
good neighbors for a moment,
and these were my thoughts--

canada,
(home of the maple leaf)--
   maple, (very fitting indeed),
a leaf from the hard-wood, with
the sweet center, that thrives in
harsh weather . . . truly a hearty
tree, in a hearty land--

--best wishes a--

(mf)

Monday, June 6, 2011

--mending benches--

every so often on our campus,
someone tips one of our special
stone benches of higher learning--

i take a certain joy in righting
them . . . like a young arnold
schwarzenegger between classes--

what is learning, without some
exertion . . .

--best wishes--

(mf)

HOLIDAYS

MONDAY, DECEMBER 27, 2010

--new beginings--

well, its new years(in a few short days),
i was thinking about the holiday while i was
walking today . . . here's what came to mind--

new years,
    ladies night, a time to celebrate finding
someone special, or for managing to hang onto them
for one more year(ladies *know* the good ones
get away . . . all too often)--
    it's a night of misty eyes, and tender kisses,
dreams realized, with the touch of the *one person*
you desire to hold you, at *exactly* the moment
you want to be held . . . magic . . . nuff said--
    but, there's another side of the story, rarely
told, about the ball dropping, and finding ones-self
alone, maybe a bit drunken, with a hair-full of
confetti, and a heart, disappointed . . .
    well, for those in despair this year, i say,
take a *deep* breath, shake that off your head, and
be patient! cause i *assure* you, there's that one,
special person out there, made *just* for you,
somewhere . . . perhaps right next to you, but with
someone who doesn't "*get*" him-or-her, quite as
deeply, or completely, as only *you* can--

"one persons trash can be another persons
happy-ever-after(so to speak)", besides, if you're
going to be miserable and alone, make it classy . . .
smile if you're up the creek--

so, have a happy holiday . . .

--best wishes to all--

by the way, i just want to thank "kristen stewart"
aka(Njang28612), for inspiring me to start this blog--

--still waiting--

"prince tippy"

(rd)

WEDNESDAY, DECEMBER 15, 2010

--the point--

some of this came to me while i was
scraping my windshield this morning--

winter--
    a change of seasons, a time
to huddle together, to find comfort,
be it brief or otherwise--
    the bitter cold hasn't *quite* the bite
of loneliness and despair . . .
    like the gifts, but love the giver,
that's christmas . . . that's the point, if
there ever *was* any, in my mind anyway . . .
    santa's bag has *lots* of goodies, but
it's *love* in the bag, not stuff--
santa's got his own kind of cool, that
can't be topp'd, duplicated, or impersonated . . .

  --he's an original--

        --merry christmas everybody--

(rd)

Thursday, October 13, 2011

--halloween--

something i wrote last night about
the up-coming holiday--

--all-hallows-eve--
a night for kids, candy, and family
fun, with hopes of no tricks, and *all*
treats . . . not even one--
for those grown, a night to cut-loose,
and "let your hair down" . . .
for ghosts, goblins, witches, and trolls,
to come alive . . . *all* over town--
for *everyone* to enjoy the *thrill* of being alive,
till morning, when a new day arrives--

--stay safe, and best wishes--

--prince tippy--

(mf)

COFFEE TALK

Friday, October 21, 2011

--coffee--

something i wrote this morning,
in one of my favorite spots--

coffee,
a small thing, that's big *all* over
the world--
a little bean that does big things . . .
getting us going *every* morning,
keeping us awake, alert, and *warm*
from within--
making the human condition better,
everyday . . . whether by yourself, or among
friends, it's a simple pleasure that remains
the same, each time--
giving comfort, and a little happiness,
to *all* . . . till your cup runs dry--

--best wishes,
prince tippy--

(mf)

MONDAY, SEPTEMBER 20, 2010

--my point of purchase friend--

this is something i wrote for a barista, who made me feel like the world was an good place to be . . . at least when she was close by--

she, and a few other "ladies of the coffee bean", are the greatest(and i think they know it too)--

--much love girls . . . much love . . . :o) --

--my point of purchase friend--

i hope this card helps convey my appreciation for what you do, each day, that helps me get going in the morning--

it's rare to meet a person who personifies the word "good", without making an effort, or to have someone warm you from the inside-out, with a look that says, "i hope you're doing ok this morning" . . .

what's even more miraculous, is that the *whole* process of making my day, takes less than one minute--

--i really appreciate it--

best wishes . . . :o)

(mf)

SUNDAY, AUGUST 7, 2011

--people watching--

something i was thinking today while
i was sipping coffee--

we are *all* used to the rich and
famous having fans, i have a unique
habit of becoming fans of everyday
people--
all of them are totally unaware of
said admiration, but it would be awkward
if they were . . . being the secret fan-base of
someone who rings up your order, or takes
your money, when you pay for gas, is a special
joy i call my own--
a lot of people don't see what's great about
them, because they don't see themselves like the
rest of us(or the person's obviously good qualities
escape everyone but me), watching someone, and
really listening, brings sights, and sounds, that inspire
the mind, and move the soul--
it's about loving someone, not for what they can
give you, but for *who* they are, and *how* that makes
you feel--

--prince tippy--

(rd)

MONDAY, JULY 11, 2011

--blowout--

had a tire blow while i was filling the
silly thing with air today . . . i wasn't using a tire gauge--
(always use one that is calibrated, and has a
"cert" from the good chaps in london . . .)

blowout . . .
   a *very* sudden deflation of
possibilities, that must be overcome
immediately--
   a test of a person's resources, *and*
resourcefulness . . . if only *all* life's
difficulties were as simple as "lefty-
loosey, righty-tighty"--
   there is a certain joy, in finding
solutions to the problems that come
to bear throughout the day, both my
own, and others(finding the answer for
a friend, brings a happiness i can only
begin to describe)--   :o)
   so, *enjoy* your flat tire . . . revel, in the
triumph of replacing anothers . . .

                --best wishes--

(mf)

TUESDAY, AUGUST 30, 2011

--*family*--

wrote this very recently, just found
a moment to post it today--

everything, the *main* thing, come
hell or high water, through *thick* and
thin, blood . . . thicker than water(if the
blood be kindred)--
stick with your loved ones . . . and your
friends who are like *them*(both *close*, and
well trusted)--
--stay sharp, keep fit, make good decisions--

--prince tippy--

(rd)

WEDNESDAY, MARCH 23, 2011

--the lead climber must not fall--

   i was getting myself squared away
this morning, and an old adventure came
to mind, kind of a saab story . . .
the north face,

   i reached the top, paused
 for a moment, and repelled down,
tethered to a friend(i wouldn't
know how tightly for many years)--
   those that climb this way aren't
conquering a mountain, or a fear
of falling, but over-coming trust
issues, and a fear of close connections--
   yes, these climbers sometimes fall,
not one, but two . . . together, or not at all--

--good hands, good heart, much love--

         --best wishes--

(mf)

SATURDAY, JANUARY 8, 2011

--the high life--

   i was getting to know a new
place the other night, which resulted
in some great conversation, and a
hi-spirited "doodle-off"(i emerged
victorious), after my win,
i wrote this--

     --(the high life)--

   the beer flows smoothly, the
bar-tender listens truly, at the bottom
of the glass, things seem better . . .
till morning . . . two aspirin and a shower,
and it's *all* good--

(mf)

Thursday, July 21, 2011

--employment--

i am looking for work again
today, i'm living in my car, penniless,
for the third year in a row . . . but i'm not
out of self respect(i just don't micro-
manage well)--   :o)

finding the right place, as a
breadwinner, to win the bread,
is an issue for all--
where we choose to work, and
what tasks we perform, have deep
meaning, and profound influence, for
the lives we lead . . . be they sparse, or
overly abundant--
working for a fool, is a fool's errand,
a good employer enhances the life of
both his customers, and the hired help,
your "boss"(seen correctly), is most
certainly another breadwinner, same as
you or i . . .
so, win the bread, somewhere you
are respected, at an honest rate--

--suffer no fools, in the office or the
break-room--

                    --prince tippy--

(mf)

MONDAY, JULY 11, 2011

--*power grab*--

a good description of someone doing the wrong thing, *exceptionally* well--

i prefer to accept what's earned, through honourable means . . . but this term describes another process entirely--

the question seems to be, what is most important, what you have, or how you attained it--

i feel it's the latter . . .

--prince tippy--

(mf)

Monday, July 25, 2011

--intent--

something i wrote sipping
coffee on saturday--

some say an action with no
intention is an empty motion,
poetry . . . with *real* wisdom--

your intention(what you had
in mind), is *so* very important, be
it giving gifts, doing a favor, or
just lending a hand, the good
intentions are the real gift--
give good intentions freely,
weigh carefully the decision to
share the ones that are not--
it's not where we go that shapes
us, it's how we get there--

--go in a good way--

--prince tippy--

(mf)

FRIDAY, JULY 15, 2011

--something special--

a few thoughts that came to me
yesterday . . . dealt with today--

something special, describes a
thing, person, or place, in good standing
with you, me, society as a whole--
a good thing used wrong, lacks
special qualities, to me . . .
take care of a special thing,
and use it in an honourable way, so
it remains special in all our eyes--

--a fool and all things are soon parted--

--prince tippy--

(rd)

TUESDAY, JULY 12, 2011

--catch 22--

my thoughts a few moments ago--

"catch-22" . . .
    a clever way to describe
someone in a situation(that is
not favourable), no matter *what*
course of action is chosen--
    today, i only hear it used to
describe something some clever
person has manufactured(for another
person to endure)--
    what glory, and honour, is present
from such pursuits, is neither obvious,
or desirable to comprehend . . .

                --prince tippy--

(mf)

THURSDAY, AUGUST 11, 2011

--enemies--

something i wrote last night while in
my favorite coffee shop--

i once heard a person say "if you
don't have any enemies . . . make some"--

sounded strange, but it's half right,
how you handle someone with bad
feelings about you, *actively* doing you
harm, builds character, and is a real
learning experience--
the tree that bends does not break,
but a bent-over tree bears little fruit . . .
be patient, until both you, and your
adversary, grow tired of it--
then, when enemies are dealt with,
the justice will be just . . .

--prince tippy--

(rd)

MILITARY

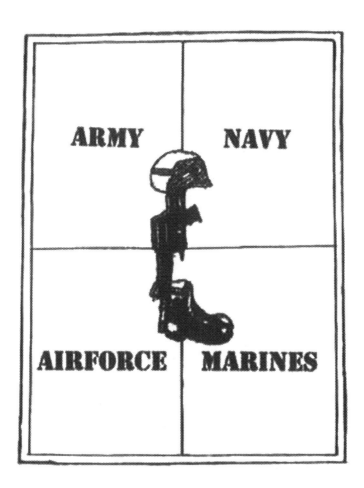

ARMY   NAVY

AIRFORCE MARINES

MONDAY, OCTOBER 10, 2011

--museum of science and industry--

    i recently had a good visit at the museum of
science and industry--

    a great way to spend some time, learning
new things, and viewing the worlds *many*
wonders . . . *all* in one place(truly a miracle)--

    i had some luck in the flight simulator(pulling
a sortie, in a little bird called a "phantom"), I
emerged with a(*small*, but silly) grin, and a few
choice foolish words, i can't recall, but my *first*
thought was, "it was *windy*" . . . although none was present--

    took a tour of another exhibit i had not seen for
awhile(1984), she was sitting quite different this time,
different, yet *still* both *amazing,* and an enigma . . . i looked
closely at the first capsule to be launched into space(seemed
like close-quarters in that single-seater), "houston . . . we
have a problem . . .", all-in-all a great visit to the "windy city",
and the museum did *not* disappoint, in any fashion--

  --stay sharp, keep fit, make good decisions--

              --prince tippy--

(rd)

MONDAY, SEPTEMBER 20, 2010

--the veterans museum--

i went to see the veterans museum in my town
a while back, here's something that came to mind
when i was there--

is it the terrible things one man can do to another,
that makes him a man?
or is it the things he can do *easily*,
but doesn't(out of *kindness*), that makes him great?--

i believe it's the latter, but that's me . . .

(rd)

Monday, September 20, 2010

--thank-you card for veterans museum--

    this is a note i sent(with a card i made), to say thank-you,
to the good folks at the museum, after my visit--

hello,
    i recently visited the museum, and i just wanted
to say, my experience there was excellent in every respect,
it brought back memories of my grandfather, who was
in the second world war--

    he was a *great* man, and served his country well, while
i was viewing one of the exhibits, a group of young people
came along, and someone was telling them about the war,
and weapons in that room . . . at that moment, i thought it would
be *great* if my grandfather could say a few words to them--

    he passed away some time ago, but i learned a lot from him
when i was young, by watching what he did, and how he did it . . .

    so, if he could, i think this is what he would have said about
the service . . .

    i wrote it down on this card, and if you could read it to *just*
one group of young people, i would be very grateful--

(rd)

Monday, September 20, 2010

--why we serve--

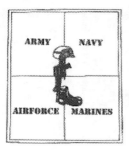

this is the card i sent(with the note to the museum), after my visit--

--why we serve--

as you walk around in here, the weapons and other instruments of war are interesting to look at, but, along-side all that stuff, are the warriors, the *main* reason to come here . . .

it's about them, it's about who they are, and why they serve, so, why do they do it? who are they? what happens to them? . . .

first of all, people don't join the military so they can learn how to kill people, they join because they're thinking they can help somebody, and a person like that, is a beautiful person . . . right?

well, they take this beautiful person, and send them somewhere *truly* horrible, and they tell them to "do the right thing", which is why a lot of them come back a little mixed up--

but, it doesn't have to last, and that's partly up to you, if you know a person who has served, maybe a relative, or a friend, show your appreciation for their efforts to keep you safe--

be understanding . . . maybe sometime you might be having breakfast with someone like that, and when you ask them if they want some more pancakes, they don't answer right away . . . it could be they're back here, in one of these rooms, in a firefight, or some *other* tough situation, that war provides--

after the moment passes, you can take their hand, or just touch them, to tell them you love them, or that you care, that you *know* where they might have just been--

if you do that, they might not come back here quite so much, or when they do, it won't be for as long . . . at the very least, on memorial day, you should go to the parade(if you can)--

if you do, when the veterans go by, take off your hat, and cover your heart, or salute(if you want to), because they deserve it, and it *really* means a lot to them . . .

--best wishes, and god bless--
(bill hawley)

(rd)

Friday, November 18, 2011

--i have a dream (military version) --

some silliness that wizzed
through my head awhile back . . .

  I have a dream . . .
there are many like it, but this one
is mine--
  though i may walk through the valley
of the shadow of death, i fear no evil,
for my dream is with me . . . and the action
is clear--

--ooh rah--

Monday, July 25, 2011

--pawns--

a few words about my love for
things both small, and *often* under-
estimated(but not by me)--

  noble pieces, at the front
line, fully in the fray--
  i always cherish the little
pieces, as well as the big,
each pawn can be queen, if
the fate of the fight makes it so--
  yes, they move slowly . . . but
deliberately, and give *all* in trade,
for the one they make war--
  the value of a piece able to
change the game in a single move,
is beyond measure--
  so often, great things come in small
packages . . . move slowly, choose wisely--

--prince tippy--

(mf)

WEDNESDAY, NOVEMBER 23, 2011

--action--

something i was thinking
yesterday--

the way of the sword . . .
    the point does the deed,
the end of the handle makes
the call--
    all the cuts come from the
same place, the blade need feel
no shame, when the duty is done--

--prince tippy--

(mf)

Saturday, July 23, 2011

--shaken, but not stirred--

a cool description, but it's
about more than what mr bond
drinks--

valour amongst stressful situations,
quick thinking, yet choosing wisely,
making it look *easy*, when those
with experience *know* they are not . . .
wielding what powers are present
within, gently, while being both soft,
and well spoken, with heavy hands
that change history, to suit the will of
the mind that moves them--
a man's man, who is a class act . . .
(a hero admired by men, *loved* by women)
a standard of man, i *try* to reach . . .
(as best i can)--

--prince tippy--

(mf)

FRIDAY, NOVEMBER 11, 2011

--duty--

something else i wrote the other day--

duty . . .
 my country, my family, my friends,
myself--
always, all the time, and in that order . . .
 a purpose, greater than myself, that i
pursue for honourable reasons, with my
whole being--
 --stand tall, think quick, stay safe--

--ooh rah--

(rd)

WEDNESDAY, JANUARY 11, 2012

--women and children first--

a few weeks ago, i was thinking
about home, and old customs,
that i both miss, and highly value,
here's what came to mind--

women and children first . . .
sounds cool, because it's the
right thing--

so, why is it these days i'm always
seeing them last in line, where are the
gents, the dudes with the sack to stand
and wait, for noble reasons . . . gentlemen . . .
the guy that knows, having grace,
and good manners, takes great strength
and good nerves--
throughout history, the man most loved,
and lusted after, has been a brute, with a
princes charm--
--be tough, act smooth, keep it real--

--prince tippy--

(rd)

TUESDAY, NOVEMBER 23, 2010

--still standing--

there was an article in the paper the other day,
about a soldier receiving the congressional
medal of honor(i think it's about time someone
won it who's still standing from this war)--

the paper printed some of what he said while
receiving it, he said he was angry his friends had
to die for him to be honored with a medal . . .
that says a lot, i think it tells us, that when
another person gives their *life* for you, that's
a gift above *all* gifts, one you would never dream of
asking for, and when you *receive* it, you want like
hell to give it back, but you can't, and that's the rub--
he said very much with few words, a trait often seen
in serviceman--
the tip of the sword never rusts, it stays clean from constant use,
and hard times, though it be strong, we keep it in a high place,
away from harm, remembered with great pride . . .
(he *really* deserved our highest honour)--

--best wishes--

(rd)

THURSDAY, JULY 14, 2011

--The CMH--

my thoughts after watching the
latest presentation--

another member of an exclusive
club, who's entry fee is both high, and
hard won--
a long war on terror, with two men,
still living, who's shoulders bear our highest
honour--
all have fought bravely, two wear the
pendant, honouring all who have served--

--ooh rah--

(mf)

Monday, September 20, 2010

--vantage point--

i wrote this for a card, to a friend, after her husband passed, whom i also knew well--

vantage point--

when we see the best in all things, each one shines--
this is the way to see the world . . .
and when we *see* it this way, all our good sides lighten the shadows on our fair natures--
the good, and the better, on the same face . . .

(mf)

i said a toast for him later that evening as well, here goes . . .

--to *all* my friends who couldn't be here, both *on* the earth, and in it . . . much love--

THURSDAY, NOVEMBER 17, 2011

Friday, November 11, 2011

--home--

something i wrote days ago, and
just found time to post--

home,
    for some it's a place, for
others it's where you happen to
be standing, and *who* you are with--

    for me, it's the latter, never mind your
surroundings, it's all about good company,
great times, and warm feelings--
    a good home invites good friends,
creates special memories, and makes
lasting connections--

--happy holidays--

--prince tippy--

(mf)

TUESDAY, AUGUST 30, 2011

--your place--

a few thoughts i just had, posted
right now--

your place,
  where is that, is it a *good* one,
and are you in it by yourself--
  be it *hell*, heaven, or just in
between the two . . . how the time
there is spent seems like the *whole*
deal--
  spend it well . . . share the parts that
seem like heaven with whom-ever
you can--
--be yourself, love another, keep it real--

--prince tippy--

(rd)

Saturday, January 22, 2011

--tears--

i was watching television one time,
and saw something that *still* hits a nerve
whenever i think of it, here's what was on--

it was a talk show, i forget who's, but
they had this servicemen on stage, with his
wife *belittling* him, for having trouble
readjusting to life without a war . . . she said
all he did was cry all the time, couldn't hold
a job, wasn't a man, merely a big child(no
wonder elvis shot his tvs sometimes)--

i don't yell normally, and almost never
at inanimate objects, but i *wanted* too that
day . . . if you ever *do* see a servicemen crying,
that's *good* news . . . it means society has got
something left to work with, it means he's
not all used up inside, and maybe, one day
he could be more than a trained killer, which,
despite his wife, and the audience's, *amateur*
opinions, is exactly what he *is*--

    it means if he had to tear your head off
for his country, in the line of duty, he might
feel something, on *some* level, someday . . .

  --hell slips away, but not on anybody's
time-table . . . you got to *wait* for a soldier
to come home(awhile after he's back)--

            --best wishes to all--

(rd)

Saturday, October 23, 2010

--running on empty--

   i was thinking about my mom this morning, over
breakfast, and this came to mind . . .

   when we are boys, men are full of hope and
trust, love comes easy, and moms mean everything,
it seems were *so* full of good feelings, it spills out
at every turn--
   but there's bumps and deep holes in life's many
roads . . . so, the tank gets low, from leaks, spills,
and awkward moments, at a point, it runs dry,
and the *true* meaning of "all used up" is realized(lean
on feelings, and bloated with experience)--
   mom's not always around to fill the tank, with a hug,
or a kind word . . . when she's gone, who fills the tank?,
and if *no-one* does, what use is an empty vessel no
body wants to fill, but won't throw away?
   i try to see the best in whatever i'm looking at,
and that's how i get by, but it's not the same . . .

--prince tippy--

(rd)

TUESDAY, JULY 12, 2011

--point blank range--

something i wrote this morning,
at my favorite coffee spot--

danger close, in your face, right
here, right now--
such is the way of living in the present . . .
dealing with what's right in front of you,
no yesterday, no tomorrow, it's about
today--
what minute are you spending right
now . . . how well is it being spent, spoiling
the now with yesterday, seems foolhardy--
but we do, all the time . . .

--enjoy the now, right now--

--best wishes--

(rd)

Monday, July 11, 2011

--in coming--

something i was thinking a
moment ago--

incoming . . .
    bad news, scream'in in, a good time to deploy
the "grab-ass-hope-for-the-best procedure",
whether you are stateside, or on a tour, enlisted
personnel, or no, it's the *same* drill . . . keep your head,
stay cool, never, ever, panic--
    hysteria produces poor results, with frightening
consistency--

--ooh rah--

(rd)

MONDAY, NOVEMBER 14, 2011

--1000 yard stare--

some thoughts i had the other day--

alone,
   by yourself in a crowded
room, people *all* around and not
a spot to think, get your head squared
away, and mingle--
  too much food for thought gags the
social life, yesterday keeps messing up
 today, very regularly--
  going moment to moment without caring . . .
someone *will* reach you, when, whom, and
where, is a mystery--
       --keep paddling--

            --prince tippy--

(rd)

SATURDAY, OCTOBER 9, 2010

--loss--

rough day today, long walk, soar feet . . .
(this came to mind along the way)--

loss,
   a condition of knowing, not having, and
enduring both, in some way--
   as we adjust to this situation, over time, the
strain is less, as the burden becomes lighter,
from *gained* strength, rather than a lightened
load . . .
   let's hope one day we might lay down this
weight, and come to a peace with how things
are, they might have been, and the way we
think things should be . . .
      --(pain fades, but love remains)--

                     --best wishes to all--

(rd)

TUESDAY, APRIL 3, 2012

--despair--

despair . . . a lack, of many things, mainly positive
thinking, brought about by sustained rough
conditions(an unofficial websters definition)--

where are you going, and what do you think there
will be when you get there . . . what, and how, you feel, can
be greatly affected by whom you are touched--

stay out of the reach of unhappy others, find joy in what
small things you can, from your actions, and your intentions . . .
wait *not* for these things from others, but take it upon yourself,
with a clear head, and a strong back, to make a world of difference,
to all--
--stay sharp, keep fit, make good decisions--

--prince tippy--

(rd)

FRIDAY, JULY 8, 2011

--hard luck--

wrote this while enjoying a
coffee, at my favorite spot here
in town(i love those ladies of the
coffee bean)--

the school of hard knocks,
learning the hard way, tough luck,
so many *ways* to describe things
not going well--
be that as it may, on the bright
side, things are still, *indeed*, going . . .
onward, to even greater heights
of despair, or, most likely, happier
times--
some of the joy of the trip, is the
bumps in the road . . .

--go in a good way--

--prince tippy--

(rd)

FRIDAY, JUNE 3, 2011

--the right thing done wrong--

i happened upon something on the
side of the road in town today, that
made me pull over--
 sometimes you've got to stop, check
your head, and reflect . . .

 they had a stone for every person
lost so far during the war on terror . . .
no names, not one--
 how do you forget something like
that? . . . i can not--

--best wishes--

(mf)

MONDAY, JUNE 6, 2011

--crapping out--

   this is something that came
to mind yesterday, after a walk--

   the dice, we all roll them, the
outcome can be joy, or hard times,
a miracle, or tragedy, going for it is
just like that--
   yes, it's true you can't lose what
you don't put in the middle, but great
men *know* it's not what's in the middle
of the table that counts . . . it's about
going for it--

        --carpe diem--

(mf)

THURSDAY, AUGUST 18, 2011

--sit-rep--

    still a homeless bum, living in my van,
down to my last three or four dollars,
can't find a job, and bills are piling up,
can't seem to stay clean(from clothes
smelling so bad), on the bright side, i am
enjoying writing and crafts(i have a lot of
free time in my current situation)--
    also, i am experiencing life at the bottom, as
a person whom people apparently feel has no value . . .
quite an experience, i may be the better for it,
at some point, but not today--(more later)

sit-rep,
    "telling it like it is", flat-out . . . and straight-up--
not for help, but a warriors "lay-of-the land",
so those in your corner *know* what round you
are fighting, and what punches have landed--
    the current state of affairs *must* be known,
before improvements can be made, whether
out-loud, or to yourself, the value is there--

--stay sharp, keep fit, make good decisions--

                  --prince tippy--

(mf)

SATURDAY, JULY 23, 2011

--A-O-C--

wrote this last night while sipping,
coffee in a local restaurant--

taking a break from it all,
in grim surroundings . . .
no umbrellas in your mia-ti,
making due with what you've
got, when what you *have* happens
to be a tad less than your worst
nightmare--
the silver lining of "A-O-C", is there
is still an "A" on the "C", forget where
you fell . . . remember when you got back
up, the greats keep going, that's how
we roll--

--ooh rah--

(rd)

THURSDAY, AUGUST 11, 2011

--roughing it--

something i wrote last night, when
an old adventure came to mind--

alone with your thoughts, close
quarters in hard times, sometimes
your troubles are not far away, you're
insulated from them, but not by much--
it's when the best you've got better do,
with luck, some good gear, and a friend . . .
you get through--
--keep calm . . . stay warm--

--prince tippy--

(rd)

Sunday, January 23, 2011

--strength--

i wrote this over a good cup
of coffee, in a *very* comfy shop
in my town, i was inspired by a
quote from a good book(on
their message board)--

nerves of steel, heart of gold--
the *rarest* combination of
humanity, unlocking the best
in everyone that person has
touched, loved, or known . . .
breathing new life where
there is loss, and new hopes
where there was none--
be that person for somebody,
as best you can--

--best wishes--

(rd)

MONDAY, JULY 11, 2011

--don't sweat the small stuff--

i wrote this a few days back,
but couldn't post it(as the library
was closed)--

the small stuff . . .
   everything, is small stuff . . .
dropping the ball is bad, not picking
it up is the real failure--
   "when the going gets tough . . .
the tough get going", or at least
moving again--
   how we handle what goes south,
is what makes us great--
   so, live and learn, be a student of life,
and remember, "it's the *first* duty of each
student, to survive the lesson"--

--best wishes--

(rd)

SATURDAY, JUNE 25, 2011

--going the distance--

wrote this last night, posting it today
to honour someone special--

to dumb to know when to quit, and
to stubborn to throw in the towel, *all* in,
all the way, committed . . . fully, in every
way--
be it for love, or country, or both,
whatever the reason, the person is
getting there, and *having* it . . . how is
not an issue-
--the will finds the way,
when the heart's all in--

--prince tippy--

(rd)

TUESDAY, SEPTEMBER 20, 2011

--when the going gets tough--

the tough get going . . . in a good way,
in the right direction--
    we all get upset, hurt, and angry . . .
for how long, and how much, depends on
whom is hurting, and how the hurt
 happened--
    let emotions flow . . . feel them fully,
and let them float away--
    when you let hard feelings go, there's
room for better things . . . like love, joy, and
happiness--

--prince tippy--

(rd)

FRIDAY, JUNE 24, 2011

--picking up the pieces--

something i was thinking about
yesterday--

a bad moment, rough luck, good
things gone bad . . . shattered, it happens,
we may not like it, but that's fate, destiny,
or something else entirely--
how we handle picking up the pieces
and what we choose to do with what's
left, is the whole deal--
healing often happens when a new
purpose is found, something mended is
something special . . . to me--

--best wishes--

(rd)

Sunday, February 27, 2011

--coming up short--

wrote this today at the mall,
here's what i was thinking just
a moment before i made a new
friend--

sometimes despite our best
efforts, what we want more than
anything is out of reach, lost, or,
doesn't want us--
how we come to terms with
this hard truth, can determine
our future a great deal--
lonesome bitterness, or
peaceful solitude . . . grim choices for
the heart, the road to bitterness
is paved with "what if's", and
"why not's", the other way is
seeing with *wise* eyes, the
good times had, and the good
feelings remembered--

--best wishes--

p.s. what i just wrote is easier
to read than to put into practice--
(but i'm workin' on it)

--prince tippy--

(rd)

MONDAY, MARCH 5, 2012

--slight-of-hand strength-of-mind--

something i wrote the other day, that i was unable
to post until this *very* moment--

"when you take the pebble from my hand,
you will *know* to ignore other people's foolishness"--

action, reaction(the wants of others, and their wishes) . . .
if they be for malice, one person *moves* the other, only when
neither is in harmony--
be yourself, instead of who a broken person wants you to be . . .
another broken thing trashing the place--

stay centered, react well, in a genuine way that fits the moment,
and nothing more . . .

--best wishes, prince tippy--

(mf)

TUESDAY, AUGUST 9, 2011

--hard feelings--

an off moment last night led me to
these feelings--

unmet expectations, slighted, unwanted,
or just not over it yet, moving past being treated
badly can take awhile, the best cure is being
treated fairly, quite often--
whatever person, place, or thing that was a jerk,
matters not, knowing with *whom* not to spend time
is usually worth the expense of a little discomfort--
seen in the right light, dark times are left behind,
and *only* the silver lining remains, as a tool wielded
by a stronger person--
--go down hard, get up quick, make the best of it--

--prince tippy--

(rd)

SATURDAY, MARCH 3, 2012

--picking up the pieces (re-visted)--

some words about how a few people i
think about make me feel--

fixing what's broken . . . sometimes means
putting something that's fallen to pieces in
front of the right person, with the right hands,
whom has great patience, and a deep understanding
of what's being saved--

the *only* one, that can see how much *more,*
the special thing in need has left to offer . . . once righted--

--have hope, give some away--

--best wishes, prince tippy--

(rd)

TUESDAY, MARCH 6, 2012

--dancing girls--

this morning's coffee was enhanced by more than
the bagel i had--

--dancing girls--

proof, not everything in the world is completely
messed up, that in fact, something is going *very*
right . . . all in one place, and right in front of you--

endless possibilities . . . something about a person
feeling good, makes another feel better, it's a good
vibe--

--best wishes, prince tippy--

(mf)

SATURDAY, APRIL 2, 2011

--in the end--

wrote this after i paid my
tab . . . (no kidding)

the sum,
the grand total, happily ever
after--
touchdown, small-town
hero makes good . . . it's the right
ending for a hero in a bad
situation--
it's not what happens, *all* too often,
making us cheer that much louder
when it does--
--here's to making it . . . ooh-rah--

--best wishes--

(rd)

FAITH

Thursday, November 11, 2010

--faith and casual conversation--

i wrote this note to my pastor, but right now i'm
not sure i sent it--

my faith, and television, are often at odds . . . this
really shows itself in my daily conversations--
here in america, we tend to respond negatively
about a subject, if whom we are speaking to has
made a negative reference first--
i catch myself doing this often, and as i study gods
word(*filled* with love and hope), this contrast is
becoming more apparent--
when i get home, and reflect on the days
conversations, often, what i recall having said,
does *not* reflect my true overall feelings about
a subject--
for example, you may admire someone at
work, but sometimes their socks don't match . . .
during a casual conversation with someone
at work that day, the sock problem may
be mentioned--
should you blindly chime in to this negative tune,
even though you highly regard this person? . . .

this issue is very similar to the shyness i have had,
on occasion, when my beliefs have been questioned--
it takes practice(and a thimble full of courage), to
go against the grain of all things--

i hope, as whom-ever reads this, sits inside . . . i
must suggest that there are *endless* opportunities
just outside that door, where america awaits--

take a few breaths, or count to five, before
answering someone setting a negative tone--

is it *really* how you feel about the subject?,
grandmas always say "if you can't say anything
nice, don't say anything at all", grandma knows
best, *almost* every time(and with frightening
precision, i might add) . . .

so, speak the positive, and save the rest for
your prayers--

(i prayed for a new pair of socks for my friend,
instead of slandering him for it . . .)

--amen--

(rd)

Tuesday, July 10, 2012

--breaking bread--

something i wrote at church last sunday,
when i was enjoying some coffee and doughnuts, while
pondering an old custom, with great meaning, here goes--

breaking bread . . .

togetherness, a basic necessity for a sound mind,
and a strong body, yes, we can live alone, but most thrive
amongst others who value them, and wither when with
enemies, or nay-sayers--

being good company, brings good company closer . . .
be yourself, forget the past, and try to remember the good
deeds done, in your favor--

--for me, the cup is always half-full if someone else is pouring--

--best wishes, prince tippy--

(rd)

Monday, July 25, 2011

--communion--

something i was thinking this
morning--

communion . . .
   reaffirming your beliefs
among friends who feel the
same--
   the custom is very personal
for each christian . . . for those of
other faiths, or none at all, a
gathering of like-minds, symbolically
showing agreement, with the principals
of the group, is(i hope), understood
and respected--
   communion happens between *you*
and god, none other are in-between,
the church provides the bread, and
the wine, in a place among friends--

   --best wishes, and god bless--

                    --prince tippy--

(rd)

Monday, May 23, 2011

--prayer request--

last sunday's prayer request, and
question for the pastor--

prayer request--
please say a prayer for my neighbors,
as they see me in a way i do not, when
i'm away from the mirror each day--

--best wishes to all--

question--
why . . . all the time, everyday, sometimes
answered, sometimes not, the *only*
question . . . for all time--

--prince tippy--

(mf)

MARTIAL ARTS

WEDNESDAY, AUGUST 24, 2011

--the martial arts (bushido)--

something i wrote less than
an hour ago--

snapping clothes, flowing like
water, with both subtle force, and
extreme power--
wielded with gentle wisdom, and
great honour, little known, yet fully
respected . . .
--honour, duty, friendship--

--prince tippy--

(mf)

SATURDAY, AUGUST 6, 2011

--the jinga--

noticed a person just before close
at work last night, that i sensed might
be a capoeta practitioner, this led me to
these thoughts about this style, and those who
pursue this type of excellence--

the heart of capoeta beats strongly
in brazil . . . the jinga goes forever--

(mf)

ROMANCE

MONDAY, SEPTEMBER 20, 2010

--my dream-girl wears chuckies--

something i wrote for a personal ad,
that got tampered with, somehow(i had to re-post it)--

she's tender, but mostly to me--
she's slender, but she doesn't see--
she's generous, so much, it makes me smile--
she's beautiful, and i love her style--
she's a lady, and she loves me--

(rd)

WEDNESDAY, NOVEMBER 16, 2011

--Njang 28612--

you crossed my mind today,
it was a pleasant passing . . .

   just the right one,
sometimes you just *know*, right away,
but the moment passes, and
something *truly* special, meant *only*
 for you, slips from your grasp . . .
   gone, but not forgotten, in case
fate favors a second chance, at something
wonderful--

--prince tippy--

(mf)

Saturday, February 19, 2011

--*waiting*---

    this came to mind yesterday,
just before work-- when i *really*
needed it . . .

    waiting . . . the noble act of being
patient to the point of bursting,
of wanting, with the deepest sincerity,
and yet humble enough, to wait . . . for
just the right moment--
  showing respect for what's desired,
love for what's wanted, and patience,
within the soul--
  making the moment we receive
what's worth waiting for, *truly*
special . . .

              --prince tippy--

(rd)

MONDAY, MARCH 7, 2011

--destiny--

   i wrote this the other day--
its kinda mushy(even for me),
but i think it's cool--

destiny--
   when the right women meets
the right man, *nothing* can
keep them apart, nothing,
they were "meant to be",
and so they shall wed--

      --best wishes to all--

(rd)

THURSDAY, JUNE 16, 2011

--deja' vu--

my thoughts this morning over
breakfast, my food stayed down, the
past didn't--

sometimes a special person comes
along and reaches you deeply, like none
other . . .
someone who connects with you
like that, is around many corners, in the
people we meet, and some of the situations
we encounter, not far from our minds, though
they may not be near in person--
feelings from the heart, reach the head at
odd times, and in strange ways . . . feels like,
magic--

--fries and coffee--

(rd)

TUESDAY, MARCH 22, 2011

--paris--

mon cher,
j'ai offert ma vie 'a la le'gion,
mais ils ne l'auraient pas--
  sur le train je vous ai donne'
mon coeur, mais le destin ne
l'auraiat pas non plus . . .
  votre gentillesse et baisers
au revoir sont toujours sur
mes joues quelquefois--
  nous aurons toujours paris--

        --tippy--

(reno)

Monday, September 20, 2010

--women are like wild flowers--

i wrote this for *all* the special women in my life thus far,
whether they know it or not, they are never far from me,
in my head, and in my heart--

--women are like wild flowers--

women are like wild flowers, because the *beautiful* part, what
you can see, isn't what makes it special--
it's the roots, the *heart* of the flower, the place where *all* that
beauty comes from, that's important--
see, not every women is a lady . . . it's not *who* she is, or how
much money she has, it's *how* she is, and how she carries herself,
that does--
a person like that, shows us *all*, that if you value yourself, other
people will too . . . she's inspiring--
anyhow, young men are in a real hurry to do everything . . .
so, when a young man sees this beautiful wild flower on the side
of the road, he's more than likely going to just *pick* it, and run home--

but before too long he's going to notice it's changed, and he'll put it in some water, or something, to try and fix it . . . not long after that, he'll see it's gone, he's messed it up--

but, a *wise* man, that happens upon that *same* flower, will be *amazed*, he *knows* what the world is like, and he can't *believe* something so beautiful could exist out there all by itself, and he'll worry someone might come along and harm it--

this man realizes, it's the *root* that makes it what it is . . . so, he'll get just the right pot, and find *just* the right soil, and the *perfect* tool, to *ease* it out of the earth--

so, when he's all set, at the *last* moment, he'll hesitate, he's a brave man, but he's scared to death he might harm this flower--

in the end, he's just got to have it, and so he takes it home, so they can always be together . . .

it's worth noting, that these wild flowers have a *peculiar* habit, of planting themselves on the roads that lead to the houses of men they like--

but the truth is, there's been *scarce* few men, that have *ever* gotten the flower home without messing it up . . .

--a lady's heart is a *special* prize, only one person in the *whole* world can claim, and that's why *true love,* is a kind of miracle, when it happens . . .

--best wishes, and god bless--

(rd)

SATURDAY, JULY 30, 2011

--besties--

a cool word i hear ladies use sometimes,
"best-friend" is how i describe the situation,
but, "besties" rolls off the tongue *really* well--

a modern term, for someone who's
"got your back", even when you look
stupid--
everybody else may walk away, but
this person's shadow will *always* be
keeping the *sun*, and *every* other of gods
creations, off your back, and *you* out of
harm's way(as best they can)--
being that person for someone else is
serious business . . . and one of my favorite
things to do in this world--

--lately i am less able, but i'm working the
problem--

--prince tippy--

(rd)

SATURDAY, JULY 23, 2011

--soul mate--

something i wrote last night when
a friend came to mind--

  your soul-mate,
    just the right person, that makes
everything better--
    the days are brighter when this
person is present, joy . . . just add
him or her, and it's had--
    a human tuning fork, that moves you
at the core(when they're close by),
two ships from the same harbor, sailing
best side-by-side, catching the same
wind, sharing a course leading to
happy times, and fond memories--

          --prince tippy--

(mf)

FRIDAY, APRIL 1, 2011

--getting checked out--

i was in a bar finding the
bottom of a few drinks, when
this came to me--

getting "checked out" . . .
  an eerie feeling, like in a
scary movie, *totally* unaware
of your situation, until you
get the sinking feeling you're
"man-candy", in a room full
of sweet-tooths . . . a modest man's
total panic situation--
  man up, and go down smiling,
most girls are gentle . . . :o)

--prince tippy--

(mf)

MONDAY, JULY 16, 2012

--the language of love--

something i was thinking yesterday, about one of the
universal ways we relate to each other--

the language of love,
   the words are less the point, as the tone--
heart-felt words, even if miss-spoken, often ring
true . . . if the person you are speaking to loves you well,
the *best* of what you said will be heard--
   so, tell those you love, that you do, as openly,
and often, as you can--

> --best wishes,
>   prince tippy--

(mf)

Tuesday, July 26, 2011

--secret admirers--

a few things that made me
laugh to myself last night--
a quick "ladies love-interest spotters
guide"--
if there is no drool present(sometimes
it runs out), a man head-over-heels for
you, or another girl standing right behind you,
will *actually* listen, to what you are saying,
while staring at your body--
he cares if you have a sniffle, aren't
dressed for the weather, seem upset,
takes up hobbies, or interests you have,
generally is *not* a jerk, smiles like he
thinks it's free . . . (he's right), and he likes
you--
anyway, that's all the "man-sense" i can
divulge without having to kill anybody--
(this message will self-destruct in five seconds)

--special agent cupid--   :o)

(mf)

WEDNESDAY, JULY 13, 2011

--wanting eyes--

something i wrote yesterday in
the park--

if a man's lucky, things go
just right, and he's paying attention
when it happens(usually he isn't), he
might see something magical, few men
ever notice--
a woman, when she realizes she
loves a man, wants his children, the
whole thing, you're the "total package",
will look at you, with *wide* eyes, and a
stillness to her face, she loves you . . .
and she's wondering (how did that happen),
but she doesn't think it's a mistake--
a special moment . . . listen to your lady,
look her in the eyes, often, so you won't
miss it--

--prince tippy--

(rd)

TUESDAY, AUGUST 9, 2011

--peas and carrots--

something i wrote last night at one
of my favorite coffee spots--

some of the foods in the basket
go good together, one thing that compliments
the other, *very* well, and *very* often--
two things that are good together, making
one thing that is great, for all time . . . peas and
carrots, a legendary pair, that have no equals
in the cookbook of history . . . they were *made*
for each other--

--prince tippy--

(mf)

SATURDAY, AUGUST 27, 2011

--the gift--

something i wrote a few days back
but was unable to post till now--

great effort made for another,
solely for the purpose of honouring
who they are, and what they mean
to you--
a ring, a poem, a task . . . something
worthy--
love expressed openly, and in a way
special to the giver, and whom given,
creating good feelings, and a lasting
connection . . . for *all* time--

--prince tippy--

(mf)

MONDAY, JANUARY 10, 2011

--valentine's day--

i was talking to someone about our
next upcoming holiday the other night,
and here are my thoughts about it today--

--valentine's day--

kind of a neat holiday if you ask me,
it's one from way, way, back . . . steeped in
tradition, romance, love, and affection--
a day to reveal affections unnoticed, or
to reaffirm old ones, still going strong . . .
people typically send cards, candy, or
flowers(for good reason)--
because i think *sending* a women flowers,
in the days of yore, *meant* something, it
does not today--
a gentlemen gave a woman flowers
to let her know he had solved a problem
for her, vanquished an enemy, dragon, or
released her from an ivory tower--
it meant he was looking out for her
interests, i believe it was known as a *favour*,
if she accepted, she accepted his protection,
and his courtship--
women did not give flowers to men, but
sometimes placed them in their hair, perhaps
to let the gentlemen know she might accept a

flower from him, or maybe to publicly display
she had received one from the gentlemen
accompanying her--

   also, the color of the flower was of a *certain*
meaning, white(for friendship), yellow or pink(for
a love interest), and red was for lovers--

  candy, candle-light dinners, love letters, poems,
and other fine treats, were usually made by the
giver . . . very romantic--

   the modern technique, of putting it all on the
charge card, just doesn't seem as sweet a gesture,
to me . . .

  so, what happened to change these traditions
i wonder(could it be more than the dragon/ivory-tower
deficit)??, or have we changed culturally this much?

   i *really* miss the little meanings, of the flowers,
candy, and so forth, it made things *so* much more fun . . .

  would you give a white flower, or another color?, a
poem, or dinner for two? . . . *anything* could happen--

   anyway, i wish everybody the best of luck,
capturing that *special* persons attention, and to the
lovers . . . a *glorious* celebration, of what you already
have--

             --a happy valentine's day to all--

(rd)

MONDAY, SEPTEMBER 20, 2010

--love happens when you're not looking--

i wrote this for a valentine's day open poetry reading,
at one of my favorite coffee shops(on valentine's day)--

--love happens when you're not looking--

love,
   it's nature's practical joke, the cosmos's wet-willy, or
perhaps an *unwanted* set of rabbit ears in your yearbook photo . . .
very personal, and *very* unexpected--
   this kind of magic is made with the heart, *waved* as a wand,
given to another, *without* expectations, or fear of rejection--
   it matters not, *whom* we love, so much as *how* we love them,
the deepest lovers cherish the *whole* person, for better, or for worse--

   today is the day we tip our hats, to those *lucky* few,
who have found each other . . .

       -- a happy valentine's day to all :o) --

(rd)

MONDAY, MAY 23, 2011

--love struck--

  i was thinking about things in a
quiet place today, and this came to mind--

  when someone *really* reaches you,
gets you, and *still* wants you, above *all*
others . . . love has struck--
  a happy blow, that heals wounds,
instead of creating them, a bolt of joy,
that runs deep . . . and lasts forever--

--prince tippy--

(rd)

TUESDAY, JULY 26, 2011

--*love story*--

something i was thinking yesterday--

a love story . . .
 it could be yours, so many
stories, one for each couple--
 make yours a *true* love story
(i am anyway), that means the
right one might not seem right to
your friends, your parents, or the
whole "bleeping" world . . . but right
for you, in your heart-of-hearts, is
the best choice--
 so many settle, or have to "press-on"
after missing the right one, fate can be
both cruel, and kind . . . be bold, and
with-hold no love from your heart's
desire, no matter what anyone else thinks--

--prince tippy--

(mf)

Wednesday, January 19, 2011

--magic--

  this time of year, a man thinks about
the special women in his life, the ones
that got away, and the *one* that made
it all better--

  people say, "you never know what
you've got till it's gone", maybe . . . cause
you never know how much you have
inside, till it dies--
  and for some(those that knew what
they had before it was lost) . . . emptiness,
going through the motions of being alive
without caring . . . it's a spell rarely broken,
but sometimes, that *one* special person,
breaks through, taking you to a place
where there's life, love, and happiness,
forever . . .

    --magic--

(rd)

TUESDAY, JANUARY 25, 2011

--commitment--

sometimes you just know . . .

commitment, a forsaking of
all other options, for the *one*
thing, way, or person, that *must*
be had--
    not from lust, greed, or envy,
but the soul . . . *knowing* when the
perfect person, path, or way, is
right in front of us--
    not a choice, but a natural
reaction to fate, no regrets . . .

        --prince tippy--

(mf)

WEDNESDAY, JANUARY 19, 2011

--tradition--

valentine's-day got me thinking,
about love, marriage, and its many
traditions . . . here are some of my
thoughts--

i have watched a few movies,
and heard tales of runaway brides,
or groom no-show nightmares . . . it
occurred to me last night, this may
be due to the loss of some ancient
traditions, that still linger today, in
small ways--
some of this is guess-work on
my part, but i think i'm on to something . . .

first off, the brides-maids were not
merely good-looking friends of the bride,
in the old days, before the availability of
toothbrushes, hair extensions, plastic surgery,
and what-have-you, a good-looking spouse
was a *hard* thing to find . . . let alone, a cutie
with a good job--
so, if a lady was in love, and to be wed,
it was the *duty* of the brides maids(and her
family), to watch the groom, the cake, and
all other aspects of her big day . . . so *nary* a
glitch was to be had--

you see, back then(and maybe today),
another jealous person, might place a burr
in the horses saddle, or loosen the wheel on
the carriage, or rub a toad on his face the
night before--
　　although the bride and groom weren't
to see each other(prior to the wedding), the
brides-maids didn't take their eyes off him,
the *whole* day . . . i imagine the level of sophistication
those ladies had put the secret service to
shame, even a hundred years ago--
　the grooms-men had a similar job, to watch
the bride, and thwart trickery, or mishaps, *of*
any kind(because there *might* be some) . . .
　the custom of the father walking his girl down the
aisle, is to be *sure* she gets there(and to the
right man) . . .
　　and the grooms *"best* man", wasn't exactly
his *"best* friend", he was his *"scariest* friend",
he *defended* the occasion, and upon the preacher
asking for any objections, he looked around the
room, to see if there was, and *helped* that man
find his seat(or the front door . . . if needed), he guarded
the wedding-night after the ceremony as well, to
make sure the deal "got sealed", *without* interruption--

so, if your future spouse didn't make it to the wedding,
you should *sit* back, and let the fact *soak* in,
that you don't have any *close* friends(and neither
does the person you are trying to marry)--

if a woman decided to elope, her lady-friends
got involved, got the best horse, checked the saddle,
packed her things, and *found her man*--
all that aside, at the wedding, *even* if everybody
showed-up, a *brave* lady had the *right,* to speak her
peace, uninterrupted, when the preacher asked(sometimes
resulting in a wedding disaster)--
that's why it's a *miracle*, anyone, *ever* successfully gets
married, falls in love, or *even* dates(in the present day), if
your one-true-love is amazing . . . somebody else may have
noticed too, game on--
--cupid's got too many arrows sometimes--
(it's best not to be jealous, but wise to be aware . . .
to *trust* . . . and *be trusted,* is the only way)--

anyway, for all those lovers getting married over the
holiday . . .

--congrat's, and best wishes--

(rd)

TUESDAY, AUGUST 9, 2011

--what if--

a few thoughts i had last night--

a slip, wrong turn, missed the
boat, that ship has sailed, what if . . . *mostly*
hurts, what *if,* is best replaced with what *now*--

now . . . living in the present, yesterday melts
away when now is *both* better, *and* appreciated,
a love lost is rekindled when there is love today . . .
not based on years past--
the touch of that *one* special person is felt for a
moment, waste *not* these precious seconds on
yesterday, where you have been, who you think you
should be, or hard times filled with bad memories . . . joy,
and enjoyment, lie in letting the past go, and now happen,
naturally--
feel joy . . . savour now, live well--

--best wishes, prince tippy--

(rd)

WEDNESDAY, JULY 13, 2011

--ripe--

    wrote this in the park yesterday
as well--

ripe . . .
    a description for fruit, folks, or
situations, that describes something
seasoned, just the right amount, or
something ready to become what it
was destined to be--
    women in this stage of life, stir a
man in a special way, feelings of home,
and happy times, children not yet born,
or that he has--
    whether the lady is his wife or not, a
respect, and warmth, is felt(in most men) . . .
all of the time--
    (turquoise and purple ladies)

--prince tippy--

(rd)

MONDAY, MARCH 7, 2011

--some nugs of wisdom--

learn to love yourself--
study other people--
earn trust--
spend it wisely--
fall in love--
raise the bar--
make a difference--
be yourself--

     --prince tippy--

(mf)

Printed in the United States
By Bookmasters